E SCIENCE

FREAKY STORIES FROM BENEATH THE SEA

BY CAITIE McANENEY

Gareth Stevens
PUBLISHING

Please visit our website, www.garethstevens.com. For a free color catalog of all our
high-quality books, call toll free 1-800-542-2595 or fax 1-877-542-2596.

Cataloging-in-Publication Data

McAneney, Caitie.
Freaky stories from beneath the sea / by Caitie McAneney.
p. cm. — (Freaky true science)
Includes index.
ISBN 978-1-4824-2964-0 (pbk.)
ISBN 978-1-4824-2965-7 (6 pack)
ISBN 978-1-4824-2966-4 (library binding)
1. Ocean — Miscellanea — Juvenile literature. I. McAneney, Caitie. II. Title.
GC21.5 M384 2016
551.46—d23

First Edition

Published in 2016 by
Gareth Stevens Publishing
111 East 14th Street, Suite 349
New York, NY 10003

Copyright © 2016 Gareth Stevens Publishing

Designer: Sarah Liddell
Editor: Ryan Nagelhout

Photo credits: Cover, p. 1 (waves) RYGER/Shutterstock.com; cover, p. 1 (anglerfish) Darlyne
A. Murawski/National Geographic/Getty Images; cover, tail used throughout book
Morphart Creation/Shutterstock.com; cover, background throughout book, p. 27 Franco
Banfi/WaterFrame/Getty Images; pp. 5, 7, 9, 11, 13, 15, 17, 19, 21, 23, 25, 27, 29 (hand used
throughout) Helena Ohman/Shutterstock.com; pp. 5, 7, 9, 11, 13, 15, 17, 19, 21, 23, 25, 27,
29 (texture throughout) Alex Gontar/Shutterstock.com; p. 5 Rich Carey/Shutterstock.com;
p. 7 Getty Images/Staff/Getty Images News/Getty Images; p. 8 Ken Usami/Photodisc/
Getty Images; p. 9 Dante Fenolio/Science Source/Getty Images; p. 10 Stasis Photo/
Shutterstock.com; p. 11 Koji Sasahara/Associated Press/AP Images; p. 12 PhotosByChip/
Shutterstock.com; p. 13 (octopus) Teguh Tirtaputra/Shutterstock.com; p. 13 (sea krait)
sciencepics/Shutterstock.com; p. 13 (stonefish) Cygnis insignis/Wikimedia Commons;
p. 14 A Cotton Photo/Shutterstock.com; p. 15 Editor at Large/Wikimedia Commons;
p. 17 Ethan Daniels/Shutterstock.com; p. 19 Jason Edwards/National Geographic/
Getty Images; p. 21 John Lund/Photographer's Choice/Getty Images; p. 23 Prioryman/
Wikimedia Commons; p. 25 (inset) Handout/Handout/Getty Images News/Getty Images;
p. 25 (main) Shin Okamoto/Moment/Getty Images; p. 29 Barcroft/Barcroft Media/
Getty Images.

Printed in the United States of America

CPSIA compliance information: Batch #CS15GS: For further information contact Gareth Stevens, New York, New York at 1-800-542-2595.

CONTENTS

Words in the glossary appear in **bold** type
the first time they are used in the text.

DISCOVERING THE DEEP SEA

There's a place in this world that's almost completely unexplored. It's home to between 50 and 80 percent of all life on Earth. We've yet to unlock its great mysteries or truly understand the science that lurks beneath the surface. We may never know all that goes on in this amazing hidden world—the ocean!

Saltwater bodies such as oceans and seas cover about 70 percent of Earth's surface. Let's dive in and explore colorful coral reefs and migratory mammals such as dolphins and whales. Travel even deeper, and you'll find a frightening assortment of creatures living in a pitch-black **habitat**, waiting to be discovered. Read on to learn about some of the freakiest features, creatures, and discoveries in the deep blue sea.

FREAKY FACTS!

The Atlantic Ocean is 27,497 feet (8,381 m) deep at its lowest point, the Milwaukee Depth inside the Puerto Rico Trench. A trench is a long, narrow cut in the ocean floor.

SCIENTISTS HAVE STUDIED THE OCEANS FOR CENTURIES, BUT THEY SAY 95 PERCENT OF OCEAN WATERS HAVE YET TO BE EXPLORED.

CORAL REEFS

Coral reefs are home to more than 2 million species of aquatic life around the world. These shallow-water habitats feature colorful fish, plants, and ancient coral. But did you know that coral reefs are actually made of *skeletons*?

FREAKY FRILLED SHARK

The frilled shark looks like a freaky sea monster. It has 300 needle-sharp teeth. It has rarely been spotted, as its usual home is the ocean floor at depths between 390 feet (119 m) and 4,200 feet (1,280 m).

The frilled sharks that have been found grow to around 6 feet (1.8 m) long, but may grow to be longer. Their bodies resemble an eel, with six pairs of gills.

For hundreds of years, the frilled shark remained a sea monster myth. However, over the past few years, there have been more human encounters with it. In 2007, a frilled shark was found off the coast of Japan in shallow water. It died hours after being captured. In 2015, a fisherman caught a frilled shark off the coast of Australia.

FREAKY FACTS!

In 1880, Captain S. W. Hanna caught an eellike shark, which might be a relative of the frilled shark. It was reported to have been 25 feet (7.6 m) long!

LIVING FOSSILS

Scientists consider frilled sharks to be living fossils. Living fossils are living species that appear similar to those found in fossils. They usually have no other species that resemble them still living, suggesting that they haven't changed much over time. The frilled shark can be traced back 80 million years, to the Cretaceous period. There's been little change to its body, and it still looks like something out of **prehistoric** times.

DEVILS
OF THE DEEP

The deep sea is home to many freaky-looking creatures that will never see the light of day. These creatures have adapted to life in the deep sea. Some glow in the dark. Others have razor-sharp teeth they use to battle it out with other deep-sea predators.

An anglerfish called the black sea devil lives deep in the Atlantic Ocean and is rarely seen. There are more than 200 kinds of anglerfish, the females growing from 8 inches (20 cm) to nearly 40 inches (102 cm) long. They have a gaping mouth full of long, sharp teeth. The female anglerfish has a body part that looks like a fishing pole, which holds a **photophore** containing glowing bacteria. Male anglerfish are tiny, and they attach themselves to a female until they fuse together. This is how they mate!

GIANT SPIDER CRAB

FREAKY FACTS!

The deep-sea giant spider crab is possibly the largest arthropod on Earth. It can grow up to 12 feet (3.7 m) from leg tip to leg tip.

FIERCE FANGS

The anglerfish isn't the only deep-sea creature with sharp teeth. Found more than 5,000 feet (1,524 m) underwater, the viperfish is a fierce hunter with fangs too long to fit inside its mouth. Though it's only up to 2 feet (0.6 m) long, the viperfish can swallow huge meals. The fangtooth has the longest teeth in relation to body size of any fish. It lives deeper than any known fish in the ocean—up to 16,000 feet (4,877 m) underwater!

AN ANGLERFISH CAN OPEN ITS MOUTH WIDE ENOUGH TO EAT PREY TWICE ITS SIZE!

TALES OF SHIP-EATING SQUIDS

In the 12th century, Norwegian sailors told of a monster squid they called the Kraken. This creature became a great Norwegian myth, and in the 18th century, there were still stories of how this monster could take hold of a ship with its **tentacles** and drag it down into the water.

The real animal that may have inspired these stories is the giant squid, or possibly its cousin, the colossal squid. Giant squids normally grow to about 33 feet (10 m) in length, but one was found to be 59 feet (18 m) long!

A giant squid's eyes are nearly 10 inches (25 cm) across—the largest eyes of any animal on Earth.

FREAKY FACTS!

The giant squid is among the largest invertebrates on Earth. Invertebrates are animals without a backbone.

WHILE THIS DEEP-SEA DWELLER DOES HAVE EIGHT LONG ARMS AND TWO TENTACLES, IT WOULDN'T WANT TO CAPTURE A SHIP. IT MUCH PREFERS EATING SHRIMP, FISH, AND SMALLER SQUIDS.

GIANT SQUID ATTACK!

In 1870, French writer Jules Verne wrote a novel about a submarine journey called *Twenty Thousand Leagues Under the Sea*. In one scene, a giant squid attacks the submarine, killing a crew member. In 2003, French sailors were competing for the Jules Verne Trophy for fastest nonstop journey around the world in their yacht, the *Geronimo*. They reported that a giant squid attached to their yacht and slowed them down!

VERY VENOMOUS

Coral reefs are amazing habitats. So many different animals mean there are plenty of fish to snack on—and many more to watch out for. Some animals have developed defenses to keep them safe from other animals and to help them catch their prey. One of the most deadly defenses is **venom**.

The blue-ringed octopus lives in shallow reef waters, staying close to the sandy floor. Its soft body and eight arms are usually a tan color, but when this octopus gets scared, bright blue rings glow all over its body. When it glows, the blue-ringed octopus is warning predators to get away while they can. This octopus can deliver a bite with enough venom to kill 26 adults within minutes. The venom **paralyzes** the octopus's victim until it can't breathe.

FREAKY FACTS!

Puffer fish are known to expand their bodies when they're scared. But they're also famous for being one of the most poisonous fish in the sea. One puffer fish has enough poison to kill 30 people if the wrong part of it is eaten.

PUFFER FISH

BANDED SEA KRAIT

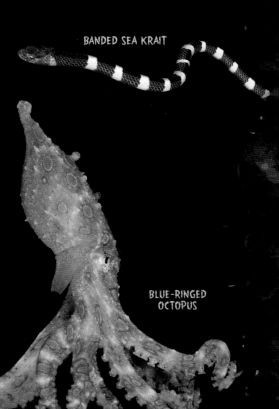

BLUE-RINGED
OCTOPUS

SNAKE IN THE WATER!

What's that slithering through the coral reef? It's a snake called the banded sea krait. The banded sea krait can live on land and in the ocean. The sea krait's black-banded body is a sign to prey to watch out. This snake is very venomous! The sea krait's venom is 10 times stronger than a rattlesnake's. Luckily for humans, this snake doesn't want to bite people. It would rather eat eels and small fish.

THE STONEFISH

DORSAL FIN SPINES

VENOM

RAISED EYES

CURVED MOUTH

TAIL

FINS

ROUGH, WARTY SKIN
FOR CAMOUFLAGE

STONEFISH BELONG TO A FISH FAMILY
CALLED SCORPION FISH. THEIR DEFENSES INCLUDE
CAMOUFLAGE, SPIKY SKIN, AND VENOM. PEOPLE CAN
SERIOUSLY HURT THEMSELVES BY STEPPING ON A
STONEFISH HIDING AMONG ROCKS.

THE WORST SHARK ATTACK EVER

On July 29, 1945, the battleship USS *Indianapolis* was headed to attack its Japanese enemies. There were 1,196 men on board. Late at night, a Japanese **torpedo** hit the ship and tore a hole in it. A fire broke out. Another torpedo hit, and the *Indianapolis* sank under the water.

Nearly 900 men from the *Indianapolis* jumped into the water. They tried to stay afloat with life jackets, a few rafts, and each other. There was smoke everywhere and blood filling the water. It wasn't long before the smell of blood attracted sharks.

First, the sharks ate the dead. Then, more sharks arrived, hungry for blood as they sniffed out the injured sailors. For days, the men floated in fear as their friends were eaten, with little food or freshwater.

14

OCEANIC WHITETIP SHARK

FREAKY FACTS!

The shark species that attacked the men of the USS *Indianapolis* may have been the oceanic whitetip shark.

SHARK SENSES

How did the sharks find the bloodied men of the USS *Indianapolis*? Their sense of smell is very sensitive. Water flows into a shark's nose, and **receptors** there pick up on smells in the water. Sharks can pick up on electrical fields given off by swimming creatures. This is called electroreception. Sharks also have a sense system called the lateral line. It allows them to feel changes in pressure and vibrations nearby.

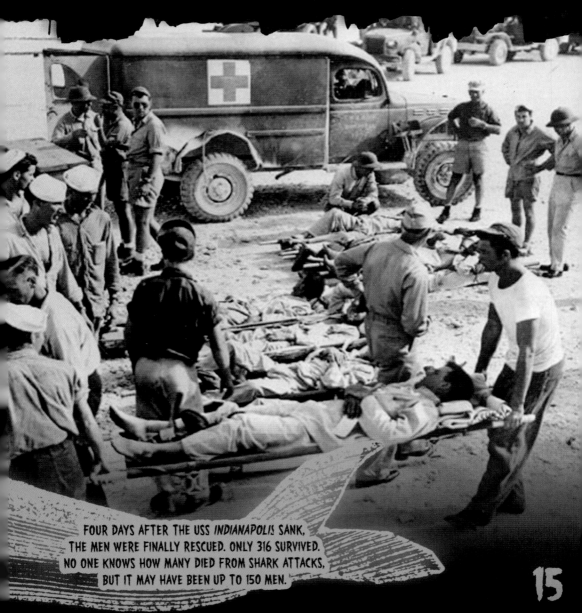

FOUR DAYS AFTER THE USS *INDIANAPOLIS* SANK, THE MEN WERE FINALLY RESCUED. ONLY 316 SURVIVED. NO ONE KNOWS HOW MANY DIED FROM SHARK ATTACKS, BUT IT MAY HAVE BEEN UP TO 150 MEN.

STINGING SWARM

Jellyfish live in oceans all over the world. They were around millions of years before fish and dinosaurs, and they'll likely outlive many species as time goes on. Jellyfish don't have brains, but they do have long, thin tentacles that can deliver a nasty sting. When these rubbery blobs get together in water, the result can be an unstoppable swarm.

Jellyfish swarms are natural occurrences, and they can be quite a sight to see. These floating "jellies" can stretch across hundreds of miles of ocean water. They may swarm for food and other resources as well as mating. This can cause major issues for humans. They can keep people from wanting to vacation on tropical coasts. They can also clog underwater pipes and nets. Their feeding can even wipe out native fish species.

FREAKY FACTS!

Even dead jellyfish and detached jellyfish tentacles can sting!

BOX JELLYFISH

The box jellyfish is one of the most venomous creatures in the world. It's sometimes called a sea wasp because of its deadly sting. Box jellyfish venom can stop a human heart in just 3 minutes. Box jellyfish live in the warm waters off the coast of Australia and in the region between the Indian and the Pacific Oceans. These clear or light blue jellyfish can grow 10 feet (3 m) long, including their tentacles. They have up to 60 tentacles and 24 eyes!

COULD CLIMATE CHANGE INCREASE JELLYFISH SWARMS? IF OCEAN TEMPERATURES RISE, JELLYFISH MAY HAVE A LONGER SWARMING SEASON. CHANGING OCEAN CURRENTS AND TEMPERATURES COULD ALSO MAKE JELLYFISH FLOAT INTO NEW TERRITORY.

KILLER CURRENTS

Imagine you're swimming in the ocean. Suddenly, a strong current tugs at you. You struggle against the current, but it pulls you away from shore. Rip currents, sometimes called riptides, result in more than 100 deaths in the United States each year. Nearly half of lifeguard rescues are due to rip currents. So what makes this killer current?

Rip currents happen when water flows from the shoreline back into the open sea. If there are obstacles, such as rocks, the water finds the easiest path around them, creating a strong current. Rip currents occur where there are breaking waves. They can move at 5 miles (8 km) per hour. Anything in their way is sucked swiftly into the deep water. Rip currents happen especially around low tide because the water is being pulled away from the shore.

FREAKY FACTS!

Rip currents are sometimes mistaken for undertows. A rip current flows along the water's surface, while an undertow is a current that flows along the ocean floor. Both can pull beachgoers away from shore.

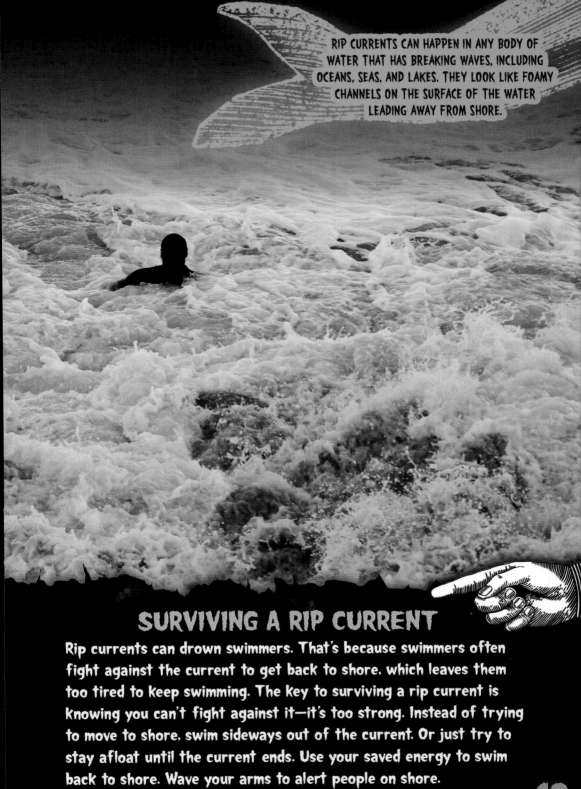

RIP CURRENTS CAN HAPPEN IN ANY BODY OF WATER THAT HAS BREAKING WAVES, INCLUDING OCEANS, SEAS, AND LAKES. THEY LOOK LIKE FOAMY CHANNELS ON THE SURFACE OF THE WATER LEADING AWAY FROM SHORE.

SURVIVING A RIP CURRENT

Rip currents can drown swimmers. That's because swimmers often fight against the current to get back to shore, which leaves them too tired to keep swimming. The key to surviving a rip current is knowing you can't fight against it—it's too strong. Instead of trying to move to shore, swim sideways out of the current. Or just try to stay afloat until the current ends. Use your saved energy to swim back to shore. Wave your arms to alert people on shore.

FREAK WAVES

Rogue waves, also known as killer or freak waves, seem to come out of nowhere. A wave is labeled as "rogue" when it grows to two times the height of the waves around it. Rogue waves can be as high as 100 feet (30.5 m)! Scientists still can't **predict** when they might happen. These waves can blow out a ship's windows, damage the deck, and even take a chunk out of the ship.

Scientists are still studying what makes rogue waves happen. Rogue waves may happen when a large ocean wave crashes into a fast-moving current. The current will focus the energy of the wave into a smaller wavelength, actually making it taller. Other rogue waves may be made when several waves combine to form one monster wave.

FREAKY FACTS!

There have long been myths about why rogue waves happen. The ancient Greeks believed that Poseidon, god of the sea, sent large waves to kill sailors out of anger.

ROGUE WAVE WIPEOUTS

Rogue waves have been recorded for hundreds of years. In 1498, Christopher Columbus's ships met a rogue wave as high as their ship's masts. The huge wave lifted his ships and dropped them. In 1853, a ship carrying around 500 people from England to Canada was wrecked by a rogue wave. The crash killed all but 102 people, who somehow made it to shore. Rogue waves have hit cruise ships, warships, and oil tankers, causing deaths, injuries, and property loss.

ROGUE WAVES ARE DIFFERENT FROM TSUNAMIS. WHILE TSUNAMIS ARE ALSO HUGE OCEAN WAVES THAT CAN CAUSE A LOT OF DAMAGE, THEY'RE CAUSED BY EARTHQUAKES ON THE OCEAN FLOOR.

WHAT'S EATING THE TITANIC?

In September 1985, a team of American and French researchers found the *Titanic*, a ship that had been lost to the sea for over 70 years. This huge ship was 883 feet (269 m) long, but it now lies in two pieces nearly 12,500 feet (3,810 m) underwater.

The researchers used remote-controlled vehicles to look around. They noticed that the ironclad *Titanic* was covered in a strange coating, like rusty icicles. In 1991, other researchers took a sample of these "rusticles" and found they were actually 27 kinds of bacteria grouped together.

One of the strains of bacteria was new and strange, named *Halomonas titanicae*. Scientists found that these bacteria were eating away at the *Titanic's* metal body over the years. The once-massive ship may someday **disintegrate**.

FREAKY FACTS!

The *Titanic* was like its own floating island with libraries, dining rooms, sporting rooms, and even a heated pool. It attracted both the very rich and the very poor.

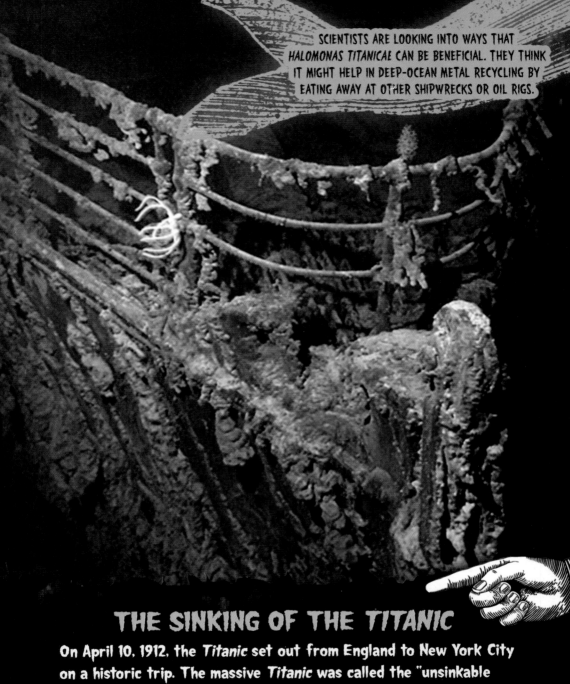

SCIENTISTS ARE LOOKING INTO WAYS THAT *HALOMONAS TITANICAE* CAN BE BENEFICIAL. THEY THINK IT MIGHT HELP IN DEEP-OCEAN METAL RECYCLING BY EATING AWAY AT OTHER SHIPWRECKS OR OIL RIGS.

THE SINKING OF THE *TITANIC*

On April 10, 1912, the *Titanic* set out from England to New York City on a historic trip. The massive *Titanic* was called the "unsinkable ship" for its new, improved design. There were nearly 2,250 people on board. On the night of April 14, 1912, the *Titanic* hit an iceberg in the middle of the Atlantic Ocean. Three hours later, the ship sank beneath the icy waters. Only 705 passengers made it onto lifeboats. The rest died in the cold ocean.

SUNKEN CITIES UNDER THE SEA

The sea has swallowed many people and ships with its killer waves and angry currents. It's also swallowed entire *cities*. Many ancient myths and texts from all over the world mention great floods, earthquakes, and rising seas. What really happened to these cities?

In 1996, archaeologists were diving in the bay near Alexandria, Egypt. What they found was an ancient part of the city, complete with statues, temples, monuments, and the foundation of a palace. It had been underwater for over 1,600 years.

Port Royal, Jamaica, is a sunken city 40 feet (12 m) underwater. Once a home for pirates and plantation owners, it was known for its lawlessness before an earthquake pulled it into the sea in 1692. Two-thirds of the city fell underwater, and more than 2,000 people were killed.

FREAKY FACTS!

Hurricanes and other storms can lead to storm surges, or the quick rising of sea levels. In 2012, Hurricane Sandy raised sea levels along the northeastern Atlantic coast. Seawater poured into low-lying streets in Manhattan, filling subway tunnels.

WILL THESE CITIES SINK?

Today, cities have to be ready to deal with the changes that may happen because of climate change. Global warming may lead to ice caps melting, which will make sea levels rise. New York City is the largest city in the United States, but it may be in trouble as sea levels around this city are expected to rise twice as quickly as those around the world. New Orleans, Louisiana, is also sinking into the ocean. In 2005, Hurricane Katrina broke many of the barriers protecting the city, causing it to flood.

NEW ORLEANS
2005

IN 1995, A 10,000-YEAR-OLD SUNKEN CITY WAS FOUND OFF THE COAST OF YONAGUNI, JAPAN. RESEARCHERS SAY THE CITY DID NOT "FALL" INTO THE SEA, MEANING THE SEA WATERS MAY HAVE RISEN OVER TIME TO SWALLOW THE STREETS, STAIRWAYS, AND ARCHES LEFT BEHIND.

UNDERWATER ERUPTIONS

The ocean floor is full of underwater mountains, trenches, and volcanoes. In fact, there are volcanic eruptions underwater nearly every day!

Each ocean has a ridge made of high mountains and volcanoes. These form where parts of Earth's crust, made of huge slabs called tectonic plates, meet and break apart. In the Atlantic Ocean, the Mid-Atlantic Ridge stretches more than 10,000 miles (16,093 m)!

Like aboveground eruptions, hot, liquid rock called lava reaches Earth's surface. However, the lava meets cold ocean water and cools to form rock. This rock, called basalt, forms a new layer of ocean crust. This crust builds to form mountains, or even islands if it reaches the water's surface. It can also cause seafloor spreading, which moves continents apart.

FREAKY FACTS!

Tamu Massif is the largest volcano on Earth. Located in the Pacific Ocean about 1,000 miles (1,609 km) from Japan, Tamu Massif's rounded dome stretches more than 100,000 square miles (258,999 sq km).

NEARLY 75 PERCENT OF EARTH'S VOLCANIC ERUPTIONS OCCUR UNDERWATER.

PLATE TECTONICS

To understand underwater landforms, you need to understand plate tectonics. On Earth's surface, there are plates floating on top of hot, soft rock. Currents in the hot, soft rock sometimes make plates crash together and form mountains. Other times, one plate will slide under another, creating a trench. When plates slide away from each other, the part between the plates opens and forms a valley. Lava comes up to fill the cracks, sometimes forming volcanoes when it reaches the surface.

MUCH MORE TO EXPLORE

The sea is full of mysteries, sunken secrets, strange happenings, and creepy creatures. There are tales of shipwrecks, treasures, and underwater cities. There are animals, like the swordfish, that have weapons on their bodies and daring defenses.

Scientists such as marine biologists, archaeologists, and oceanographers take a dive under the sea's surface to discover new things and study marine animals in their natural environment. They also work to learn more about how the ocean works and how humans can conserve marine life for many years to come. Some scientists see how climate change, large ships, and pollution impact ocean life.

One thing is certain: from the black depths of the deep sea to colorful coral reefs, from freaky underwater features to fascinating fish, we have much more to explore.

FREAKY FACTS!

The Marianas Trench is the deepest part of any of the world's oceans. Located in the Pacific Ocean, this trench is more than 36,000 feet (10,973 m) deep, and its bottom has yet to be explored by humans.

SEA SNOT

Sea snot is the name for floating snot-like blobs that clog up the Mediterranean Sea each year. They can cover over 124 miles (200 km) each summer. Sea snot is made of tiny dead and living creatures, called "marine snow," that come together. As the climate warms, sea snot season is lasting longer. It's full of bacteria and viruses that cause illness, such as a bacterium called *E. coli.* Scientists are studying this sea snot to see how it's spreading, how it affects humans, and how climate change makes it worse.

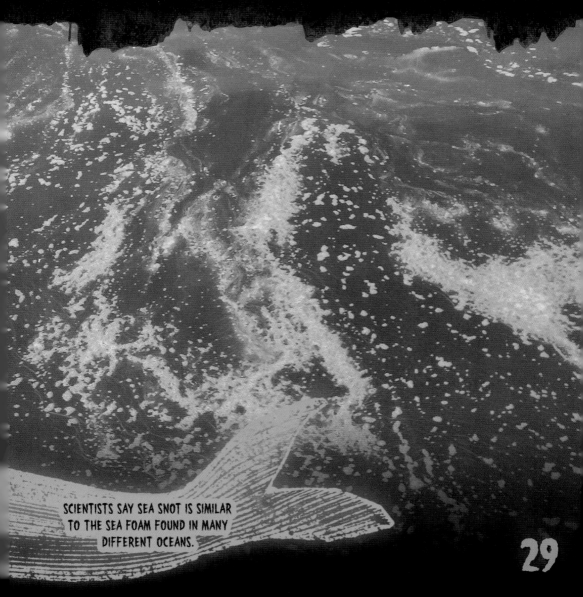

SCIENTISTS SAY SEA SNOT IS SIMILAR TO THE SEA FOAM FOUND IN MANY DIFFERENT OCEANS.

GLOSSARY

arthropod: an animal that lacks a backbone and has a skeleton on the outside of its body

camouflage: colors or shapes in animals that allow them to blend with their surroundings

disintegrate: to break apart into many small parts

habitat: the natural place where an animal or plant lives

paralyze: to make something lose the ability to move

photophore: an organ that gives off light

predict: to guess what will happen in the future based on facts or knowledge

prehistoric: having to do with the time before written history

receptor: a nerve ending that senses changes in light, temperature, or pressure and makes the body react in a certain way

tentacle: a long, thin body part that sticks out from an animal's head or mouth

torpedo: a thin submarine weapon that moves on its own

venom: something an animal makes in its body that can harm other animals

FOR MORE INFORMATION

BOOKS

Johnson, Rebecca L. *Journey into the Deep: Discovering New Ocean Creatures*. Minneapolis, MN: Millbrook Press, 2011.

Knowlton, Nancy. *Citizens of the Sea: Wondrous Creatures from the Census of Marine Life*. Washington, DC: National Geographic, 2010.

MacQuitty, Miranda. *DK Eyewitness Books: Ocean*. New York, NY: DK, 2014.

WEBSITES

Dive and Discover: Expeditions to the Seafloor
divediscover.whoi.edu/
Go on expeditions to the ocean floor all over the world and learn about exciting deep-sea discoveries.

Photo Gallery: Deep-Sea Creatures
ocean.nationalgeographic.com/ocean/photos/deep-sea-creatures/
Click through a photo gallery of deep-sea creatures to learn more about these rarely seen animals.

Spotlight: Coral Reefs
kidsdiscover.com/spotlight/coral-reefs/
Learn more about what makes a coral reef and which animals call these colorful habitats home.

INDEX